DRIVING BACKWARDS WHILE MOVING FORWARD IS INSANITY

TERESA PARKS

authorHOUSE®

AuthorHouse™
1663 Liberty Drive
Bloomington, IN 47403
www.authorhouse.com
Phone: 833-262-8899

Published by AuthorHouse 02/23/2023

ISBN: 978-1-6655-7766-3 (sc)
ISBN: 978-1-6655-7768-7 (e)

Library of Congress Control Number: 2022922694

Print information available on the last page.

As a little girl growing up in South Central Los Angeles during the sixties living in a three bedroom house my parents were loving, caring and friendly people would come to our house and it became a gathering of folks, my parents were very hospitable they would all get together and cook some food. Our family and friends were large, their kids were all over the place they chased me and my brother all around house up and down the street, my brother decided he was going to take a stand, there were about nine of them. I decided I was going to keep on running, when I came around the corner they had tied my brother to the tree. That's when I decided to find a place to hide, when the coast was clear I ran in the house my dad asked, "Where's your brother?" "Tied to the tree", I replied. I remember this one particular friend came over often, Cousin T, when he visited he would always grab me and rub his beard up and down my face the more I squirm the tighter he would hold me to him. It was fun at first then it began to hurt maybe because my face was tender. After a while I hated

to see him coming he began to tickle me I laughed so loud my mom said let her go T and go outside. I didn't like playing with the other kids they made me feel bad about myself and some of the boys would say mean things to me I felt better by myself. I was bullied as a kid especially at school I never told anyone, there were times at school it would be two or more girls talking smack to me with a crowd standing around, I never said a word. Other kids would ask me, "Why didn't you say something?" Well, I was scared I just didn't tell every time somebody did or said something to me. Things I should have told but I didn't. T continued to visit, he even brought me some birds, pigeons, one was white and the other one was blue and gray he said they were rolling birds which meant that when you threw them up they would tumble down to the ground he also brought a cage and some food. After a while he began to rub his beard up and down my face and tickle me this time his touching became inappropriate, I managed to get loose, I look into his eyes and something felt wrong so I ran into the house my mom asked did I like the birds I said yes T came in after me I still didn't say nothing.

The next time I saw T he had his son with him and other family/friends members followed behind him once again another gathering the women headed towards the kitchen to

cook this time my dad fired up the grill and they moved the festivities outside. They played dominoes, listen to music, they took turns checking the meat the women would bring pans to put the meat in. We played tag or dodge ball sometimes the women would play with us. In our backyard we had three or four big trees we call them Duke trees they were beautiful I used to just look up in those trees and just imagined myself sitting up there. One day my brother and his friends were in the backyard they wrapped a rope around one of the branches and tied a tire to it and they would swing or twist the rope till it would spin you around you had to hold on tight or it would fling you off and you could get hurt. If we fell off we got up brush ourselves off and tried it again, we also used to stack old mattresses and jump off the garage unless we broke an arm, a leg or the side of our face was bleeding a lot that's the only time we went in the house even then I was the only girl that played those dare devil games with the boys. I learned how to climb Duke trees. The following day when family/friends came to visit I would climb up in Dukes trees and hide from them I couldn't go that high just high enough where they couldn't see me or reach me they would tell that I was up in the trees and my parents would make me come down. During the sixties you didn't hear too much about sexual abuse, child abuse. When I was being touched inappropriately, I would say

to myself maybe it wasn't intentional and I'd move on. When T would tickle me and rub his beard up and down my face in front of my parents and they said nothing only when I got too loud and they got tired of hearing my mouth then they would say T leave her alone now go outside and play. These incidents happened too often with different people for a long time and my attitude began to change and I started cursing, fighting, I began to rebel, but nothing too obvious but enough to let my brother and other kids know that I had changed they didn't know why I just got meaner. I started talking to T as if I was grown, he couldn't tell me anything I knew then at an early age I had some power I had information that he didn't want to be known I learned at an young age how to used my silence to get what I want not only with him but other people too. One time Cousin T asked me to get him a glass of water I said not thinking get it yourself my mom hit me my dad said you going to get your butt beat talking to adults like that now watch your mouth my parents didn't play being disrespectful or talking back to any adult now get yo butt in there and get him a glass of water. I remember I had got in trouble and my mom told me to go outside to get a switch I went out the back door into the backyard I headed straight to Dukes trees I climb up in the tree so my dad sent my brother out there to get me when he climbed up in the tree I went higher he told my dad

that he couldn't reach me. I stayed up there later that day my dad had these friends that lived in Chicago their son came to California to visit he stayed with us for a while he became our big brother he treated me like a little sister so when I saw him coming up the drive way to enter the house through the back door I hurried down and ran toward him and jump on his back as he entered the house he had no idea what was going on or what's getting ready to happen I held on for dear life we both got a whooping that day I hated to do that to him but I was scared and hungry. T came to visit this time he came to talk to my parents his son needed a place to stay for a few days they agreed, our big brother D had found a job and moved out he still came to visit he loved my mom it was something about my mom that people loved. My brother and I was in elementary at the time T's son R came to live with us he was a little older than us, I believe he was in junior high school but he didn't go to school for some reason. We didn't see too much of him in the beginning when T was coming around so R moved in so far it was cool at first seem like he didn't liked little kids. Everything seems to be going well my parents appeared to be comfortable. We only had one tv and it's in the living room we had to agree on what to watch so we did, he says alright guys it's time for you guys to get ready for bed so I said you are not my daddy so we start laughing he gets up and chases us around

the house now it becomes a game we're having fun then he says okay play time is over my brother goes to his room I go to mine. After a while he checks on us and says goodnight. A few days passed and my parents goes to play cards or dominoes no problem. R is left to watch over us again same routine we're watching a little tv then off to bed, this time it was different, I was sleeping when he came in to check on me. I could feel his hands rubbing in between my legs, when I woke up he says shh. I said no, there's a noise on the front porch it's my parents he walks quickly to the living room and sits on the couch, I get up and goes into the living room my mom opens the front door there I am standing in the living room she says what are you doing up I said he woke me up he said I was checking on you and your brother I woke him up to go to the bathroom and I covered you up and you woke up, I could tell by the look on my parents face that something wasn't right my mom said come on let's get you back in bed I heard my dad say you got to go. The next day T came by to visit and my father had a talk with him the next thing I knew his son R had gathered his things and they left we didn't see cousin T to much after that his visits became less and less.

My parents continued to entertain family and friends. If only I had told them the things that was going on with me and

other family/friends, the outcome would have been different. I believe the relationship between my parents' family/friends would have been destroyed. My mother wouldn't have gotten over the hurt and disappointment of the actions and behavior displayed from the people she loved, knew and trusted. I remember when my mom's best friend that lived down the street cursed my brother out, she called him everything but a child of God my mom didn't handle that well she went looking for her, I could tell it bothered her so just imagine telling her about a family member doing unspeakable things to another one of her children. My mom's relationship with her mom and baby sister they were close, closer than the other two siblings. I think because I didn't say anything people thought I was weak, no, it just made me stronger I develop a strong dislike for them I didn't trust them even though I loved them, they were family. Here I am holding on to all the abuse that I suffered at the hands of family/friends, but when it came to my brother I stood up and spoke out, but I couldn't do that for myself.

My dad was a very talented and skillful man from Mississippi with a third- grade education he would do whatever it took to protect us he didn't care if it was family or friends, my mom on the other hand came out here with her baby sister they went to and they graduated from High School in

California while the two older siblings had families and were still in Georgia. I was always a child that paid attention to grown up business when they gave little gatherings I always tried to ease my way in and help with hosting getting some ice for their drinks, emptying the ash trays ease dropping on their conversation my mom would always run me out of there she would tell me to go to bed I would always find a way to ease back in there, when they were on the floor slow dancing I would sneak and drink their drinks I didn't know what they were drinking I would just drink it, the music was playing, they were laughing and talking loud they didn't pay attention to me so I partied with them until I got sleepy and then I went to bed. The next day was just another day I went outside to play in my playhouse with my in visitable friends then D from down the street came to play with me even though he did things to me he was my friend. I played by myself a lot of times with the dogs.

Family/friends visited our house often when they got together there were always some type of activity, we would sit on the porch and they would make homemade ice cream or we would all gather up and go to long beach, they would go fishing's we would go feed the seals and sometimes we would go ride the rides at the amusement park. We would

take pictures, play the penny arcade or eat cotton candy, we would drive the bumper cars, we rode the roller coaster, we never rode the Ferris wheel, my mom liked to bowl. I enjoyed those outings especially those away from the house we didn't eat much of the food there my mom always made sandwiches or fried some chicken to feed us afterwards. We didn't want much. My dad would take us to Tijuana to get some fireworks, maraca's or we would just walk through. Thanksgiving my mom made cakes, pies, ham, turkey and all the trimmings, the family/friends would gather at our house, she would cook like that for Christmas my mom was big on those days, we would go trick or treating on Halloween sometime my mom would make up my face and dress me up in some old clothes it was fun. I hated when my mom would leave us at one of her sister's house my cousin were mean to me never my brother or they were saying things or touching me inappropriately and my aunts would let us know that they didn't have enough food to feed us.

One time my cousin made us a mustard sandwich sprinkle with sugar it was good I thought that was another way to make a sandwich. Being around my family/friends it was always some type of excitement going on, I remember my dad got into a fight with my aunt's husband he beat my dad up it was funny

the two sisters didn't say a word my mom brought my dad in the house and my aunt took my uncle home. The next day they all got together again. As a child I wasn't around a lot of females, I spent a lot of time around boys and adults. My mom told me when I was about three years old she gave me to her mom because I had horns in my forehead and my G-ma kept me for a while. Life began to change with our family my mom became a nurse my dad found steady work my brother and I didn't need anyone to watch over us which was cool I had my dogs my brother had his friends. My mom and dad visited my G-ma often. Later my G-ma was diagnose with cancer she later went into the hospital for an operation stayed a few days and was released my mom and dad took care of her they made sure she had what she needed, they cook and clean for her my mom changed her dressing I stayed with her on the weekends and whenever there was a break from school. Everyone in her the building knew me or knew of me.

We moved a lot but we never settled in to one neighborhood my brother and I never went to one school for more than one semester then we would move again. There was a strain in their relationship all communication between the two have stop. My mom was very spiritual in fact my whole family was, we were brought up in Church, her daughters

were the smartest, the most beautiful, talented and toughest women I knew. My mom carried a lot on her shoulders the cares of her was a lot. As things continued to happen with me my whole idea was to make sure my mom was alright. Things was happening to me right up under their nose and because it involved the family and even some friends I couldn't tell her or my dad. I carried that shame, the hurt and pain around day and night. I develop different personalities that helped me to cope and get through the difficult times.

The neighbor that lived next door had three daughters and one son. They would invite me over from time to time, they were the only interaction I had with girls and they treated me like a little sister. Sometimes my mom would let me spend the night, we had pajama parties, we would listen to music and dance, and they would read and tell me stories I enjoyed myself. One weekend my mom allowed me to stay over they took me to a party with them they were smoking, drinking and dancing, they didn't mine if I had drink, I even met someone I really felt like a teenager. We stayed about an hour. A lot of the habits I learned was due to the interactions with older people I don't blame them I knew right from wrong. They were my only real interaction with girls even though they were older than I was. They stayed with us sometimes, we all went to school

together well the oldest boy not the other three, the oldest was a problem in school until one day he was acting up in school and they called my mom she went up to the school took him in the boys bathroom and tore him a new one she didn't play that he was no more trouble.

My mom and dad to me was a little distance we all still stayed in the house together but it was the same. Later we experience the Watts riot that was scary people were looting, stores were being set on fire the national guard was called in to control the people we had a curfew they were checking people houses to see if they had stolen furniture or other items we had to go to other areas to shop for food my mom and dad decided it was time for us to move. We did move to an apartment things began to change between my parents people wasn't visiting like they used to that was good for me.

We moved to Compton. Things really changed we didn't see my step brothers at all my dad wasn't home much my mother was making plans to get out on her own. My dad had left he was gone for a day or so then we moved secretly. I was okay with the move even though I loved and missed my dad I was okay. My parents reconciled my mom had went to nursing school and finish became a nurse for once I thought we were

going to be okay it never was the same my dad started staying out more my mom was working all kind of hours people began to visit more and more my brothers friend took up resident and so did my cousins I was still the only female my brothers started back coming around everyone was older. My brothers started getting high and so did I now I'm into boys nothing major I'm still a virgin. My life became so dysfunctional I was ditching some classes not all, catching the bus up to other schools this one particular school I went up to with a couple of friends some girls acting like boys cornered us in the bathroom and said they were going to screw us with the umbrellas it was raining that day we literally had to fight we ended up making it out of the bathroom running across the field one of the girls that I was with didn't stay too far so I went to her house the bad thing was I couldn't make it back to my home school to get home so I had to call my mom to come and pick me up and she did boy I didn't live that down and she kick my butt. Even that didn't stop my behavior I got worse the guy that I liked like my mom but I never told her and I would lie to him about what she knew what the hell I was invisible to me I wasn't even notice unless I got in trouble and I knew how to fly under the radar my brother on the other hand they thought he was an angel straight A student a sharp dresser by brother wore slacks, thousand island shoes, big afro pencil on the side of his head

everybody liked him he wasn't a bad boys he didn't date a lot but the girls liked him me on the other hand I would pick and choose what class to go to B or C student I still didn't have any one I could call my friend everything I did I did by myself. My parents didn't know that I was getting high and dating but my brother was getting busted left and right, they bought him a car he wreck it the first day I didn't get a chance to ride in it. My mom let him drive her car he hit a lady in her car the woman curse him out so bad my mom and I went up there to see what was going on my brother told my mom that she curse him my mom asked her did you curse my son the lady said yes I cursed him my mom check her so tough that she got in her car and left and we went on our way they never said another word about the accident.

J enjoyed myself and the people I interacted with, even though it might not have been the best situation, I survived and learned. This is not some sad story, it's my life experience at its highest and the lowest point. Life is not textbook, it's not scripted then it happens that way no, when life shows up it will show you better than anyone can tell you. At this stage of my life, I learned something, I learned that my journey had just begun. I traveled through the valleys which lead me down a long and dark path. I learned that when I would fall down

it was a way for me to dodge objects, people and places, gather my thoughts, brush myself off and get back up. I became stronger and wiser in my thoughts. I was an invisible person with No direction and every time I got up, I was on a different path.

There are two roads to life, in my opinion the long and the short, and this journey was necessary. I never went through the front door of life only the back door, who knocks at the back door? Me. I was determined to be better than I thought. In my mind no one could see me anyway. I traveled down the darkest road of my life, I was living in a corrupt city (my mind) where everybody knows everyone, yet No one knew me, the scariest part was my family or friends never knew where I was at any given time. My outside activities were always looking for something that I was missing, what I was missing when nobody ever knew I was gone, I'm still invisible. I remembered one occasion I entered a room where the man that was in charged invited me in to sit at his table, he just stared at me, he began to served me with his best, he told me that he wanted me for himself, he told me how beautiful I was, the thought of being seen and admired felt good and for the first time I had an idea what it felt like to be told that someone wanted me, when I looked into his eyes I seen him for who he really was, being

invisible had its advantages I could get up at any time and walk away. I walked through a house full of people engaging in different activities, I watched people do what I thought they wouldn't ordinarily do had it not been for the drugs. I already developed many personalities to help me to cope and adapt to different situations and environments that I was in. Throughout my journey I wasn't the only one traveling this road. I had my own little red book.

I decided I was going to walk the streets to make some cash didn't work for me and besides the women out there had it down to a science, one night me and a friend went out stood on the streets trying to make a little cash them women chased us for at least five blocks we laughed for a while. I became the Queen in my own movie. I learned on my journey that it prepared me for certain situations, what don't kill you will make you stronger not smarter. My family never knew of my activities and yes for a minute I blamed them. I come from a family of strong black men and women and my life outside of that they would have killed me. I was raised in the Church I participated in every Church function, and family gathering. When I was at home I wasn't. I went to a lot of beach parties; I hung out with some of the liveliest people and somehow, I gained their respect. After a while I slowed down, I got tired of

hanging out. As time passed my parents separated and my dad wasn't coming around that much. The school semester started in September I was determined to turn my life around and make better choices and decisions. Everything was on a positive note we had moved to a nice house, my mom had steady work and we were happy.

As time moved forward, I got sick my mom made an appointment for me to see the doctor. Our doctor served the family, so he knew us. After he examined me, he told my aunt that I was five months pregnant. The father of my child was like the Invisible Man he didn't contribute nothing, my mom and I did it all with help from her mother. My daughter was three months old when I lost my mom, my brother and I became separated after the funeral, my G-ma had my daughter I went back to the streets my brother lived with family.

My journey began again. I traveled from house to house, every now and then I would go to my G-mas house to check on my daughter making sure she knew who I was praying that she recognized my face and the sound of my voice. Drugs became a part of my everyday life. I knew that I always needed to keep up with my daughter and my brother's whereabouts. I had heard that my brother was in the hospital, so I went to

see him. The doctor informed me that he needed in-home care and someone to clean and dress his wound I couldn't so my aunt took the job. I was lost with no plan and no direction. Once again, I'm pregnant, what am I'm going to do? I decided to go and talk to my aunt. She made me an appointment with her doctor and my pregnancy was confirmed. I stayed with my aunt for a few days so that I could figure things out, I overheard a conversation between my aunt and dad talking about abortions, that's when I decided to leave. I went back to the streets to stay with friends. I needed some time to think and come up with a plan. I made up my mind that I was going to move in with my G-ma and save some money so I can get a place for me, my babies and my brother. I spoke with my dad, and he said he would help us. After I had my baby, my dad found us a house once again and we were happy. Everything appears to be going great somebody drop the ball the next thing I knew we were moving to another location. For me after the move I began to feel like I had to settle in order to maintain or exist in this life. After the move my brother became employed which was good but he would lock his bedroom door and that was okay I just wanted to listen to his music but I couldn't so I would break into his room and play his music then he would set up booby traps lol. My brother stops coming home some nights, then he started dating the young lady that lived across

the street. I started dating someone. My brother eventually moves across the street I didn't see him to much after then, the guy I was dating had asked me to marry him, a recipe for disaster. My intentions were not to marry this man, I felt alone, and I was still grieving the death of my mom, now I have two little girls that depended on me. My brother was surrounded by family and friends, to me I was still alone and once again I was invisible. My dad was so against my wedding he didn't show up, really, I'm not mad. We got married, my aunt got him a job where she worked, he earned maybe two checks then he quit. I continue to support the household. My aunt gave me a car and he took control of that, in fact later down the line in our marriage my dad gave me a car also he took possession of that. My self-esteem went down to zero, later we divorce. I started dating men that was abusive physically, mentally, emotionally and financially. My life didn't get any better, I started drinking and doing drugs to make me feel, I did every drug but two all I knew was to keep getting up. After being in a dark tunnel I thought I had seen the light of day but it was only a figure standing in the shallows waiting to push me back down. I thought he was different, but he was a cop hooked on drugs. Enough is enough I met a wolf in sheep clothing. I became homeless again this time I brought my children with me. This

time I had to humble myself and asked my aunt if I could stay with her, she said yes, I was grateful.

One morning after my kids had went to school I started crying and praying to God that if He got me and my kids out of this mess He would never have to worry about me again. Happy days are here again I could see the light at end of the tunnel and not a figure. I found a job; with my first paycheck I bought bunk beds for my kids. Things began to look up. One day I met a young lady at the resource center. She gave an assessment test after I finish, she gave some paperwork to take up to one of the community colleges, she encouraged me, she told me that I was a fighter and she liked that about me. Throughout my whole entire life no one ever encouraged me to do differently. When my mom passed that's all I had wanted from my aunts to take me in, love me and make me a part of their family. This woman embraced me until I could stand on my own two feet, she showed interest and concern for me her no was no, and her yes was yes I learned to hold my head up high.

I enrolled myself in a community college, I took classes day and night for criminal justice. She would schedule me a time to come see her to see how things were going and if I

needed help with anything transportation, supplies, money for lunch or just to talk. She set me up an appointment to enroll in the Vista program where I enrolled as a volunteer with the Probation Dept. My choices in men still needed to be work on. After I had completed my courses, I finished the first half of my volunteering services with Vista and later I enrolled in Drug and Alcohol Classes and became certified. For once I felt like I was going to be okay. This journey has been challenging. I wrote this book because I struggle in life, every decision I made was a backward choice, I looked for love in all the wrong places. Instead of facing my fears, my pain and my concerns I sought other means to make me feel better. I experience rape, racism, abuse from family and friends verbal and physical, I did every drug but two. I was never on the inside looking out, I was on the outside looking in. My personality carried me through. I learned to stand on the Word of God He never left me. I joined the Church for the wrong reasons instead of looking for God I look for people I later found out they were as sick as I was.

Throughout my journey there were only two ministers that talked to me, educated me and recommended organizations that would be helpful in my walk. I've never been in rehab, never been in prison and never talked to a therapist, my only crime was not naming people that committed sexual abuse to me.

Now I'm a fighter but that's not the way, tell someone. Choose the person that would share your life carefully, especially if you have children, a boy or girl it doesn't matter. I've dated the Mack aka pimp, a traveler aka running man, a Chameleon who blends in with other crowds, a leopard that's on the prowl and worst of all Temptation aka dangerous and has no heart just to name a few. Throughout my journey I've picked myself up held my head up high dust me off and became the best that I could be. I've supervised over one-hundred federal inmates, over eighty state inmates and conducted various drug and alcohol clients, facilitated groups.

There are so many resources compared to when I was coming up, no one spoke of suicide in the sixties, drugs weren't heard of that much, sexual or child abuse wasn't heard of that much. I often wondered what it was about me that put a target on my back. I have survived the worst of the worst and I'm still standing. I spite of whatever anyone of us goes through there's a solution, drugs are not the answer, suicide is not the answer and sometimes just sometime prison saves lives depending on your journey.

There are only two roads to life right and wrong we will never be perfect, if you find yourself on the wrong path gather

your thoughts or talk to someone. There are no excuses I choose not to tell my parents for whatever reason, I carry that to this day. I believe what I went through effects my relationships today with my children, men, family and friends I know how to love I just don't know what love feels like.

Printed in the United States
by Baker & Taylor Publisher Services